Tea at Downton

Afternoon Tea Recipes from The Unofficial Guide to Downton Abbey

Elizabeth Fellow

Elizabeth Fellow

First Printing, 2014

Printed in the United States of America

Table of Contents

Introduction

Come rain or shine in Edwardian England, everything stopped for tea. Just what would our beloved Crawley household have eaten at their sacred 4 o'clock institution?

These are the recipes of the golden age of England. At the height of the power of the British Empire, Mrs Patmore would have every possible kind of delicious ingredients to draw from.

Sadly, the tradition of tea has declined over time, but recently it has enjoyed a rather elaborate renaissance.

This book takes you through the steps of how to throw the perfect tea party. From the etiquette behind how to hold one's teacup correctly to the recipe for the favourite sandwich of Queen Alexandra.

Delight all of your friends with these simple-to-follow authentic recipes, and be sure that even the Dowager Duchess would be impressed with your social graces.

From the bottom tier sandwiches to the elegant cakes of the top tier, we cover it all. Not forgetting of course the perfect scone recipe and its accompanying jams.

Follow the ways Mrs Patmore would have planned her menus to keep spending to a minimum, and you too can enjoy a most delightful repast for just a few shilling!

So, what are we waiting for? Carson has opened the door to let you inside. Let's see what's for tea!

Preface

This book is arranged into two main sections. The first is the history behind afternoon tea and how it came to be, why it flourished, and how England has nearly lost one of its finest institutions. Hopefully you, the reader, will do your bit to revive it.

We discuss how to make the perfect cup of tea, and why, in fact, the English love the beverage quite so much.

The second part of the book has the recipes. Many are taken from original cookbooks of the time, others like the Chelsea Bun and Eccles Cake have stood the test of time and have been passed from mother to daughter.

Follow the tips for etiquette of which part of the tea cup goes where, and avoid those dreadful faux pas which really one can only excuse Tom Branson from making.

Without further ado...It's time for tea.

Elizabeth Fellow

The Origins and History of Afternoon Tea:

The afternoon tea is the quintessential British tradition. Any political changes to be made by members of the Downton household are manoeuvred and strategized by the women at teatime. Unravelling their napkins one just knows there will be something of great importance discussed. But just how did it come to be, that in England "Everything stops for tea"?

Its origins date back to the mid-1840s. It is thought we owe thanks to the Duchess of Bedford, Anna Marie Russell, a lifelong friend and Lady of the Bedchamber to Queen Victoria. On a visit to the Duke of Rutland in the beautiful Belvoir Castle (pronounced Beaver) in Leicestershire, the duchess found she was too hungry to wait until dinner, which would have been served at about 8pm.

She instructed her lady-in-waiting to bring her some sandwiches and cake, which she ate in her chamber. Finding it the perfect repast to get her through from breakfast to evening, she began taking this new meal each day. Realising it could be quite jolly to collect news and chatter, she invited other ladies to join her in her own chamber at Woburn Abbey, on the border of Buckinghamshire and Bedfordshire.

The duchess was a celebrated socialite, and was famous for her love of gossip, which got her into trouble on more than one occasion. Visiting London, she took her penchant for tea parties with her. Suddenly everyone wanted to do the same. Ladies across the length and breadth of England were taking tea. As it gained in favour, so did it in respectability. Parties came out of the bedchamber and were moved to the drawing room.

In 1857, the Duchess died. Three years later Queen Victoria tragically also lost the love of her life, Prince Albert. Grief stricken, Victoria mourned, and her friends watched on sadly. As time passed, she was encouraged to start inviting friends to tea as a way to distract her from her sorrow and move back into the public eye. As the Queen took tea, so did the rest of society and the aristocracy. Now rather than the long wait from breakfast to dinner time, a light luncheon had been added and the obligatory afternoon tea.

Origins and History of High Tea

Later we will talk a little more about the beverage tea. Here, it is important to know that it was an extremely expensive commodity. Unable to afford the lavish tea, the servants and working classes wanted their own version to keep them going. In the large houses, when the tea pots had been drained upstairs, the tea leaves were used again by the servants, and then were sold at the back door.

In the Midlands and Northern England, the factories choked out black smog as the Industrial Revolution was well under way. Hungry workers came home from their jobs, and cold meats and a cup of tea were placed on the table for them to eat. At 6pm, this meal became known as high tea.

Unlike the low sofas in the elegant drawing rooms, high tea was eaten while sitting at the table. The name "High" came from the chairs on which the working classes sat. You will sometimes see afternoon tea also called Low Tea, but it is not a term often used.

Later, High Tea would also come to mean a simple meal which the family of the house could rustle up if the servants were away, something small, filling and simple.

Change of the Role of Afternoon Tea alongside the Role of Women

In some ways, the longevity of life in Britain was lengthened by the rise in popularity for tea. Since the water had to be boiled, it offered a safe drink to quaff, taking the place of the gallons of ale that were drunk each day from even breakfast time!

In Victorian Britain, women were intended to be merely decorative, as opposed to useful. A well-bred woman should be seen and not heard. In the working classes, shop girls had to renounce a career in order to become a wife. It's worth remembering that whilst the role of women has changed over time, their biology has not. Females were every bit as bright then as they are now. Many were savvy, a few were schemers, and several were astute politicians. In some ways, they knew how to "work" their men to their own ends better than we do now. Afternoon tea was a chance for the women to rally their own troops and send them back to their husbands to set change in motion.

Yet despite this newfound power, there was a rumbling underground. Fervour for change was gathering momentum. In 1897, the suffrage movement was formed and middle class women began lobbying parliament for Votes for Women.

These were educated women, with strong minds and forceful ideals. Afternoon tea was the perfect opportunity for the contagion for change to spread. It was a slow and painstaking process. The winds of change blew a little stronger as war broke out in 1914. With men taken from the workforce to the front lines, the country needed women to be employed to keep the country turning. Between 1914 and 1918, England's workforce added another one million women to its number.

In some ways the change was temporary. When war was over, servicemen returned to take back their jobs, and females were expected to resume to their more "natural" roles as wives and mothers. The 1918 Representation of the Peoples Act gave men over 21 and to women over 30 the right to vote.

For some women, the need to move forward was irresistible. They had tasted freedom, and it had been good. They no longer wanted the shackles of the trussed-up elegant frocks, their needlework, and strolls around the garden. Their active minds were thirsty for more chances to shine.

Watch the hemlines of ladies Edith's and Mary's dresses as a hint to their attitudes to work. Famously, as the roaring twenties took hold, the knee length flapper dresses declared to the world that women now wanted to become active.

As women gradually come out of the home and into the work place, it becomes harder and harder for afternoon tea to hold its place in the day. Then just 21 years after the War to End All Wars ended, Germany invaded Poland, and suddenly the women of England found themselves busy again.

Many women this time were employed on the land, ensuring the country had enough food to sustain them through the war effort. Rationing took hold. In 1940, butter and sugar were rationed, in 1941, eggs were too. Two ounces of butter, eight ounces of sugar, and one egg a week (per adult) were scant pickings for the creation of an afternoon tea. Gradually trends changed, and tradition began to peter away.

Thanks to programs like Downton Abbey, the old saying is coming true. *What goes around, comes around.* The afternoon tea is enjoying somewhat of a revival. It's down to people like you and me to ensure that it grows in popularity and can become an institution once again.

You may find it interesting to know Queen Elizabeth is said to still enjoy a slice of cake and a biscuit each afternoon at 5pm. In the Midlands, people still come home to eat tea rather than dinner, which is reserved for parties.

Cream Tea, Celebration Tea, and Royal Tea

You may also see these terms. For the purposes of clarity:

A. A "cream tea" is scones served with lashings of whipped cream and jam. The best of these are to be found in Devon and Cornwall on the south coast. As an aside, one should never add cream to the beverage, tea. Instead use milk or lemon.
B. A "celebration tea" is a tea party where there is a special occasion cake served too. Usually this is for a birthday or engagement party.
C. The "Royal Tea" is said to have been manufactured by the Ritz. It begins with Champagne and ends with sherry.

The Edwardian Kitchen and Kitchen Garden

Whilst filmed at Highclere castle, which is not far from London, the fictional Downton Abbey is set in the beautiful rolling dales of Yorkshire. In the fresh air, fine cattle roam the fields and wonderful crops grow aplenty.

Mrs Patmore and Daisy created culinary masterpieces from fine crops and wonderful meats. In addition to this, the English kitchen had the spoils of foodstuffs from around the world. At the height of its power in 1922, the British Empire held sway over 458 million people, which was then one fifth of the planet's population.

Coincidentally, it was in that very year that Lord Carnarvon, (the then-time resident of the true Highclere) discovered the tomb of Tutankhamen. The ingredients of the dishes of the time often paid testament to these well-travelled influences and fascinations.

Despite all of this, however, the evening dinners would be predominately French inspired, (due to the magic Marc Antoine Carème had created in the kitchens of George IV at the turn of the 19th century). Afternoon tea however, remained indisputably British. Downstairs meals were less fancy. The fare of the staff would be the likes of stews and hotpots (a Lancashire dish).

Seasonality

In a house the size of Downton, the cook would likely be the best paid of the household staff, followed by the Butler. As Mrs Patmore is female however, we should suspect she would have been paid around £10 less a year (around $5,000 dollars in today's money) than any male equivalent there may have been.

Required to feed not only the family but the staff too, she and Daisy would prepare food for around 30 people each day. In addition to the cooking, she would have to source produce which would keep the food bill low.

Houses such as Downton enjoyed stunning kitchen gardens laden with all manner of delicious vegetables, herbs, and fruits. Exploiting the seasonal gluts not only helped the purse strings but improved the flavour of the culinary creations too.

They would have enjoyed a wide variety of game, especially during the shooting seasons (Aug 12th to Dec 10th) and river fish such as trout and salmon.

As every good cook knows, to get the very best monetary value in a kitchen, one must use ingredients cleverly. Sandwiches, for instance, are always made from minced cold meats. Potentially these were a leftover bonus from another, richer meal. On days where the family enjoyed meringues at dinner, downstairs may have enjoyed treacle tart using the left over yolks.

One final point to consider is meals were served in the kitchen and then full plates were taken to the dining room. This meant of course, if Mrs P. wanted to squirrel away half a chicken for tomorrow's sandwiches, this was entirely under her control.

Downton and Highclere

Of all the counties in England, Yorkshire possibly has the richest tradition of cakes. Parkin, Bram Brack, and of course their famous Yorkshire puddings (originally eaten with Jam rather than roast beef) have become timeless classics.

The Perfect Pot of Tea

Tea had initially found its way to England in the mid-1600s, and was touted in the coffee houses of the time. These were dens of great thinking, political debate, and anarchy. In 1660, *two ounces of tea* were presented to King Charles II at court. He and his Portuguese wife, Catherine of Braganza, took to drinking tea in court.

The beverage was an immediate hit.

Originally grown in China around the time of Anna of Bedford's first sandwich, small tree grafts were secreted away from China and over to India. Mainly due to the efforts of the East India Tea Company, this is where most of the tea leaves of the time would have come from.

The dispersal of tea was greatly helped by the growth of the railways of the time, but demand far outstripped supply, which meant an ounce of tea leaves was an extremely expensive commodity. By the turn of the twentieth century, the price war was just beginning to level, and the Crawley household would have felt the price beginning to plummet fast.

Whilst the tradition of afternoon tea has declined, tea *drinking* is very much alive and well in Britain with the estimation that the average person will get through 1.9kg (just over 4lbs) of tea a year.

Grading of Tea

Apart from the wealth of different teas available (An Edwardian tea would always have had black tea) the leaves are also classified according to the grade of the tea. For those not familiar, tea is made from the dried leaves of the *Camellia sinensis* bush.

The finest of all teas is **Orange Pekoe**. Rather than being a type of tea, this tells us that only the top youngest buds have been taken along with one or perhaps two of the young leaves. These leaves are rolled into little balls and make a full bodied yet light tea. You will see this labelled as OP.

BOP refers to **Broken Orange Pekoe**, the second grade. This has been processed to put the tea into bags (as in packaging, not teabags!) As the leaves are broken, there is of course breakage and dust. This is the lowest grade called **Fannings** or **Dust.**

For the Dowager Duchess, of course, there would only have been Orange Pekoe.

How to Make and Serve Tea

My grandmother would tell you the best tea is made in a china tea pot where there has been some accumulation of tannin on the inside over time! At Downton Abbey, however, a clean, warmed bone china or silver tea pot was used. Water must be brought to a rolling boil and then quickly added to the leaves in the pot. The taste of a good cup of tea relies on there being plenty of oxygen in the water. Boil it for too long, and the oxygen evaporates off.

How Much Tea to Use?

Around this time, in the States, tea bags were starting to be used after silken pouches of tea were mistakenly placed into teabags in 1908. Certainly by the '20s, this was standard American way to make tea. Suggesting such a thing in

Yorkshire would, I suspect, have guaranteed you would be never invited for tea again.

For authenticity, please.....an Afternoon Tea must be made with loose leaves.

One teaspoon of tea per person, and one for the pot!

Warming of the Pot

You may have seen Violet using the most magnificent tilting kettle to add water to the teapot, only to throw it away. Here, she is warming the pot. Since the key to the infusion of the leaves is that they become very warm, this quick rinse round raises the temperature so the chill of the china does not leach the precious heat from the water.

How Long Should it Stand?

Leave the tea to steep for 3-4 minutes, and then give the pot a stir. Replace the lid securely.

Who Pours the Tea?

Traditionally the pot would have been placed by the tea boy in front of the hostess in order for her to serve to her guests. If, however, something occurred to stop this happening, then the person closest to the pot should offer to take over. The traditional way to do this is to ask the question "Shall I be mother?" One would suppose, though, this maybe a throwback to high tea rather than afternoon tea.

Always serve clockwise around the table. Pour the tea through a strainer to catch the leaves. (Those of you who have a bit of the Gypsy Rose Lee in you may choose to ignore this step and do a little fortune telling. Whilst that is a whole different book, I feel sure the Duchess would never have held truck with *"such utter nonsense."*

Adding Milk and Lemon

Historically one added milk first in order to protect the glaze of the precious cups. Therefore, adding it *after* the tea was a sign of great status, signifying that one could afford to put the taste of the tea over the cup.

Actually it has been scientifically proven that tea added to milk tastes different than milk added to tea. Apparently, the heating of the milk denatures lactalbumin and lactoglobulin. It is correct to add milk to already poured tea.

If, however, one prefers a fresher, sharper brew, then a slice of lemon can be added instead. This is particularly nice if you choose to serve Earl Grey. Do not be tempted to add both, since the citrus will curdle your milk.

Etiquette of the Teacup

Are you ready?

When tea is served at the table, one should leave the saucer on the table and lift the cup alone. When standing or sitting on a low chair, lift both. They should never be stretched more than 12 inches apart. When sitting, cradle the cup and saucer in the lap and never wave around your cup when speaking.

The teaspoon and handle of the cup should always be rested at the position of 4 o'clock.

When stirring in milk and sugar, gently move the fluid in a figure of 8 taking care not to let the spoon clink the china.

The Role of the Pinkie!

When holding your tea cup, it should rest on the ring finger, which along with the little finger, should be curled inwards. This dates back to Roman times, when the elite would eat with three fingers whilst hoodlums shovelled in food with their entire hand.

The Recipes.... from the Bottom of the Cake Stand, Up!

So without further ado, let's start thinking about creations to delight the palate. Please bear in mind the origins of Afternoon Tea were filling an appetite gap. Tea is designed to avoid the blood sugar dip, not have you bouncing off the ceiling from too much sugar. Although it can be tempting to laden plates with cakes, make it gentile and elegant, not coma inducing!

When considering what to make, here is a tip: remember Mrs Patmore would make use of what she had. Try to overlap your recipes to get the most for your money. Also, Mrs Patmore would have stored things like pastry on the cool steps of her larder so that she did not have to keep repeating the same recipes over and over again. Pastry freezes well. Make more than you need, and put half in the freezer to make another batch later.

Whilst nowadays, tiny circular cakes adorn the top tier, don't make extra work for yourself. Tray bakes work well to be cut into bite-sized pieces, or if you want to be really clever, cut out circles from them using a cookie cutter.

When judging size, consider this. Everything on your cake stand should be eaten in only two bites.

Arrangement of the delicacies should be:

    I.   Top tier: cakes
   II.   Middle tier: scones
  III.   Bottom tier: sandwiches

Sandwiches

Many hotels which serve tea will use triangular cuts of bread. The Edwardian sandwiches were rectangular fingers. Crusts were always cut off, and the ingredients are not designed to be subtle. Often they made good use of chutneys, herbs, and spices to ensure a flavour explosion in the mouth.

The sandwich was already very popular by the time afternoon tea was thought of. Legend has it the 4th Earl of Sandwich ordered his valet to bring him some meat between two slices of bread at the gaming table in the 18th Century. "I'll have the same as Sandwich" was heard to follow. It seems likely though, this was to be the beginning of the name rather than the discovery of the mighty dish!

The bread of Edwardian sandwiches would always have been thin slices from a Pullman Loaf, a square sided white tin loaf. Brown bread sandwiches are not really authentic to the period.

For the most success at "the look," create your whole sandwiches and stack them. Then, managing the pile, slice away the crusts, and cut the sandwiches into four fingers. Gathering up each stack, lay them down on your stand. This should ensure perfectly measured blocks of food, neat and very pretty.

The recipes which follow are some of the more unusual ones. Of course, ham and cheese were served, especially downstairs. The recipes are just a glimpse of more spectacular efforts. Many of these are adapted from the 1925 cookery bible by C.F Leyel, "The Gentle Art of Cookery."

Historically, to keep the sandwiches cool until required, the cook would take a napkin soaked and squeezed of cold water and lay it over.

Please note that all sandwich recipes are to make four servings.

Queen Alexandra's Sandwich

Alexandra of Denmark was married to Edward VII. She was the longest holder ever of the title Princess of Wales. On the death of her mother-in-law, Queen Victoria, in 1901, Alexandra became Empress of India and wife to the King of England.

This was the quintessential sandwich of Edwardian society.

For the flavoured butter:

5 oz butter

½ tbsp lemon juice

1 tbsp mild French mustard

For the Chicken Mayonnaise:

4 oz minced, poached chicken (page 34)

3 tbsp mayonnaise (page 30)

Sprinkle of hot sauce or Tabasco

Also:

8 slices of bread

4 slices of cooked tongue

Sprinkle of mustard cress or watercress.

First Combine ingredients for chicken mayonnaise and set aside.

Then make your butter (page 32), and coat 4 of the slices of bread.

Lay over the tongue, then a thin layer of chicken mayonnaise, some cress, and then top with the other slice of bread.

Lady Mary's Smoked Salmon and Dill

For the butter:

2½ oz (65g) butter

1 heaping tsp fresh dill

Squeeze of lemon juice

Also:

8 slices of bread

4-8 slices of smoked salmon (depends on size of pieces)

¼ cucumber (thinly sliced and peeled)

Make your butter (page 32). Spread onto the bread. Add salmon and cucumber, and then add the top slice of bread.

Lady Sybil's Creamed Chicken Sandwich

8 oz (225g) minced, poached chicken

8 oz (225g) celery

8 oz (225g) very thick béchamel sauce (page 31)

½ grated onion

2 beaten egg whites

8 slices of bread

Sauté the celery until it is softened and translucent, and add the grated onion. When softened, add the chicken and the thickened sauce.

Whip the egg whites to stiff peaks, and then combine.

Add the mix to a bain marie (page 78) and heat, but do not allow it to come to the boil. (As an indicator for health reasons, the chicken needs to reach 79 degrees Celcius (174 Fahrenheit) to be safe to eat when allowed to cool again – so you are looking for a hint of a bubble rising in the sauce).

Pour the blend into a mould. Let it cool, and set solid.

Turn out, and slice to use on your sandwiches.

Isobel's Cheese Sandwich

2 eggs

2 oz (60g) grated parmesan cheese

Anchovy Paste (page 32)

8 slices of bread

Beat the eggs and add the cheese. Cook until thickened, and leave to cool.

Spread over the bread with anchovy paste. Add the cheese mix.

Martha's Cold Devil Sandwich

8 oz (225g) minced poached chicken

8 oz (225g) celery, finely chopped

3 oz (85g) tartar sauce

8 slices of bread

Mix together, and then enjoy!

Briathwait's Devilled Salmon Sandwich

4 oz (125g) Tin salmon

2 oz (60g) Butter

Couple of shakes of Worcester sauce

¼ Cucumber

French dressing (page 33)

8 slices of bread

Pound the salmon and butter together, and season with Worcester sauce, salt, and pepper.

Dip the cucumber in French dressing (page 33).

Spread between the bread.

Mrs Hughes' Cheese and Egg Sandwiches

6 oz (140g) grated cheddar

1 hard-boiled egg

1 oz butter

1 tbsp French mustard

8 slices of bread

Blend the egg yolk with the butter. Add in the mustard. Add the cheese and spread between the bread slices.

Some Repeated Design Elements

For ease, this section covers some of the more repetitive elements which appear in the recipes. Feel free to skip straight to the next section where we discover how to make the perfect Scones and Jam (page 35).

Mayonnaise

For authenticity, you should attempt to create real mayonnaise. The taste is so much superior to store-bought. It is incredibly easy to make. Daisy used a hand whisk, but putting the food processor on the lowest setting then gently drizzling the oil into the spout is easier and far less stressful. For those who are not purists, head for the supermarket!

Don't forget to use up your leftover egg whites for virtually free macaroons.

2 egg yolks

1 heaped teaspoon Dijon mustard

17 fl oz (500 ml) olive oil

1-2 tbsp white wine vinegar

½ lemon

Sea salt

Whisk your egg yolks. Slowly add the oil whilst continuing to whisk. Stop when you have added half. Add half the vinegar to slacken the mix. Carry on again until all the oil is blended in. Season with the rest of the vinegar, lemon, and salt.

Store in a sterilised jar for up to a week

Béchamel Sauce

This is a good example of using leftovers for tomorrow's Tea. This recipe will make enough for you to serve at an evening meal or make a lasagne. Keep some back to add the most sumptuous dimension to your sandwiches.

15 fl oz (425 ml) chicken stock

10 fl oz (280 ml) milk

2 oz butter

1 oz flour

6 peppercorns

1 carrot

1 onion

Parsley and half a bay leaf

Salt and pepper

Take the stock, milk, carrot, onions, herb, and seasoning, and heat together. Bring to the boil, and leave to simmer for 20 minutes. Remove from the heat, and strain through a sieve retaining the milk mix.

Now heat together the butter and flour and thoroughly combined, little by little add the milk mix. Ensure at each stage that the milk is entirely absorbed and the butter and flour roux returns to a smooth paste. Stir well until all the milk is added and the sauce thickens. Add salt and pepper to season.

Flavoured butters

Much of the flavouring of the sandwiches is built into the butter. Unless directed, choose unsalted butter (margarine was in kitchens by then, but butter tastes so much better!), and allow it to soften to room temperature before trying to work it. Mix in your ingredients, and then replace to the refrigerator to chill and let the flavours permeate.

When it is time to make the sandwiches, allow it to soften again for ease of spreading.

Anchovy Paste

A favourite of the time, anchovy paste was often used as a sandwich alternative to butter. It is also delicious on toast.

3 oz (75g) salted anchovy fillets

3½ oz (100g) butter

A large pinch each of grated nutmeg, ground ginger, and ground cinnamon

A couple of shakes of Tabasco

Mash together well, or wiz up in the food processor.

French Dressing

1 tbsp white wine vinegar

Salt and pepper to taste

1 tsp Dijon mustard

3 tbsp olive oil

1 crushed garlic clove

You will need a jar with a lid to mix. Shake vigorously! This recipe keeps for up to week if stored in the fridge.

Minced Meat

The meat used in the recipes is usually cold broiled (poached) meat which has been minced. Daisy's arm would have been well employed turning the handle for hours, but for ease, feel free to shred the chicken or put it into the food processor. Whilst you will not get the long sausage shapes she would have achieved, setting the machine onto "pulse" gives a fairly good comparison.

How to Poach a Chicken

Even today this is the tastiest and most economical way to make your bird feed the family. It ensured every last scrap of the meat falls away from the bone and also makes a delicious bi-product of chicken stock for gravies and soups.

Place your bird into your largest cooking pot. Add in celery, carrots, onion, bay leaf, and peppercorns, and fill with enough water to cover.

Bring to the boil, and then leave to simmer for an hour and 20 minutes.

Serve hot, or set aside to cool in order to mince for sandwiches.

Scones and Jams

Basic Scone Recipe

The perfect basic scone below can be adapted adding dried fruit and spices. If adding sultanas, soak them in cold tea to plump up and avoid burning during baking. As with all baking, the weather will affect how much fluid your flour will take up. Add it little by little to ensure you make dry, easily workable dough.

8 oz (225g) self-rising flour

Pinch of salt

2 oz (55g) butter

1 oz (25g) caster (superfine) sugar

5 fl oz (150ml) milk

1 free-range egg, beaten, to glaze (alternatively use a little milk)

Preheat oven to 220C /425F/gas mark 7

Rub together the butter and flour, stir in the sugar and salt. Combine together with the milk, and gently pat into dough with your hands. Shape into a disc of around 1 inch thick.

Lightly grease a baking try. Use a cutter to cut out shapes, and then glaze with the milk or egg.

Bake for 12-15 minutes until lightly golden brown.

Remove from the oven, and place on a cooling rack. To achieve that lovely soft-topped scone, cover with a damp tea towel during cooling. For a crunchier scone, omit this step.

Jams and Preserves

To make a really great jam it is important to ensure the sugar syrup cooks long enough and hot enough for the jam to set hard. This, of course, brings dangers of scalds, so be very aware and mindful of splashes.

For those lucky enough to have a sugar thermometer, we are aiming for is 104C/220F degrees. For the rest of us, the setting point can be checked by placing a *small plate* in the freezer. When your jam has boiled for around 15 minutes, spoon a small amount onto your chilled plate. When it reaches the right consistency, you will be able to push it with your finger, and it will form a skin. If this does not happen, give it a few minutes longer.

Your pan can also influence how well your jam sets. The wider the top, the more surface area there is for evaporation, and the better the jam.

To store the jam, it needs to go into sterilised jars to avoid moulds forming. Adding hot jam to cold glass will cause the glass to shatter, so it makes sense to have the jars drying as you make the jam. Wash thoroughly in hot soapy water, and rinse. Place upside down into a moderate oven for 5 minutes to dry without contaminants. Lids should be boiled for 5 minutes. Remove from the oven with oven mitts.

Lady Rose's Strawberry Preserve

The easiest jam ever invented, and I promise you will never buy a pot from the shop again!

2 lb (900 g) slightly under-ripe strawberries

1½ lb (700 g) sugar

Juice 1 large lemon

½ oz (10 g) butter

Place your strawberries and sugar into your preserving pan, and leave overnight. The sugar will leach out all of the juice by morning. I like to leave mine for 24 hours.

Chill your plates and sterilise your jars (page 37).

Turn onto a moderate heat, and allow the sugar crystals to dissolve. When you can see no more crystals turn up to a very high heat, add the juice of the lemon (mind the seeds!), and let the mixture boil hard for exactly 8 minutes.

Do the plate test. (page 37)

If you are happy with how it has set, turn off the heat, and allow it to cool in the pan for 15 minutes. (If you pot it faster, all the strawberries fall to the bottom of the jar.)

Leave to cool fully before adding jar lids. Process for 5 minutes in a water bath.

The Countess's Lemon Curd

Makes 1 large 9 oz jar of curd

4 unwaxed lemons, zest, and juice

7 oz (200g) sugar

3½ oz (100g) unsalted butter, cut into cubes

3 free-range eggs, plus 1 free-range egg yolk

Sterilise your jars (page 37

Add the lemon zest, juice, butter, and sugar to a bain marie. Heat over the water, but do not allow the mixture to touch the water. Stir to help the butter and sugar melt properly.

Lightly whisk the eggs and yolk, then whisk them thoroughly into the mixture. As the eggs cook, the mixture thickens. When it is completely cooked through, you will be able to coat the back of a spoon, and then draw a clear line through it with your finger.

Add to the jars. Cool thoroughly before putting on the lid. This will keep for up to 3 months if kept in the fridge.

Lady Edith's Gooseberry Jam

2 lb 4oz (1kg) gooseberries, top and tailed

2 lb 4oz (1kg) sugar

5 fl oz (150ml) water

Cool your plates and sterilise your jars (page 37).

Add the ingredients to a large pan, and bring to boil. Reduce the heat, and let the fruit cook until softened.

When they have gone slightly mushy, raise the temperature, and bring the jam to a rolling boil.

Boil fast for 8 minutes. Remove from the heat, and perform a plate test. If not quite cooked, return to the heat, otherwise skim off any scum with a small knob of butter. Leave to cool for 15 minutes before putting into jars. Cool completely before putting on lids. Process for 10 minutes in a water bath.

Cakes

How to Make Sweet Short Crust Pastry (also known as Pâté Sucrée)

The pastries were the prettiest part of the tea. Daisy or Ivy would most likely have made the pastries and moulded them into tins whilst Mrs Patmore was involved in creating the tasty fillings. If you plan to make more than one set of pastries, double the amount of pastry you make and store some for later.

There is truth in the saying that cold hands make the best pastry. The aim is to work it as little as you can and try to retain some very thin pieces of butter in the mix. This is what gives a delicious buttery crunch to the finished tart. Always run your wrists under a cold taps for a few moments to cool the blood running to your hands and bring down your handling temperature. Use milk that has been cooled in the fridge.

Daisy did not have the benefit of cling film, but it is an added advantage to place your dough between two pieces. Then after chilling for half an hour, roll it out between the films. You will find it far easier to move and manage than her old way of lifting on the rolling pin.

8 oz (225g) plain flour

4 oz (110g) butter

3 oz (80g) sugar

1 large egg

Rub the butter into the flour using fingertips only. Mix in the sugar, and bind together with the beaten egg. If the pastry is a little dry, sprinkle in a few drops of cold milk.

Chill for 30 minutes before using.

Many recipes say *"bake blind"* which means the pastry needs to be baked before the fillings are added.

To do this, first turn your tin over, and shape some baking parchment to it to give a guideline as to how much it will take to line it.

Turn the tin back over, grease and mould the pastry to it. Lightly prick the surface with a fork to allow any steam to escape and make the base crisp. Put the pieces of moulded baking parchment over the pastry, and weight it down with baking beans or dried marrow fat peas.

Put into the oven to lightly bake.

How to Make Puff Pastry

9 oz (250g) plain flour

9 oz (250g) unsalted butter

4½ fl oz (125ml) ice-cold water

Start by preparing the butter. Lay it between two sheets of baking parchment, and batter it to as thin a sheet as you can.

Then cut up the butter into tiny pieces, and rub it into the flour.

Bring together into a dry dough with the water.

Wrap in cling film, and chill in the fridge for 15 minutes

Take out the pastry, and roll out into a rectangle of about 8 ins by 6 ins.

Take up the edges, and fold the pastry into three, so the layers sit on top of each other. A little like an envelope.

Turn it 90 degrees, and repeat the rolling and folding.

Turn it again and repeat.

Wrap it in cling film, and return to the fridge for a further 30 minutes.

Repeat the rolling and folding process one last time, and return to the fridge to chill for a final 30 minutes.

Anna's Egg Custards

Use one recipe of Pâté sucrée (page 41)

For the custard filling:

1¼ pint (700ml) full-fat (whole) milk

7 free-range egg yolks

3½ oz (90g) sugar

Freshly ground nutmeg

Preheat the oven to 200C/400F/Gas Mark 6.

Lightly grease a 12-hole muffin tin.

Roll out your pastry, and cut into rounds with an 11cm/4 inch cutter. Place one in each of the holes of the tin, moulding them to shape.

Warm the milk, but do not allow it to boil. In another large bowl, whisk together the egg yolks and the sugar.

Pour the near-boiling milk onto the egg mixture, stir well, return it to the pan, and boil gently. Stir continuously until the custard is cooked and coats the back of the spoon.

Pour the custard into the pastry cases.

Grate over with nutmeg.

Bake in the oven for 15 minutes, then turn the oven down to 180C/350F, and bake for a further 10.

Aim for a slight dome to the tarts, but not too large as this signifies over-cooking. If this does happen, your custard will sink in the middle. To rescue this, let the tin cool for a few minutes in a tray of cool water.

Allow the tarts to cool for around 30 minutes before gently lifting from the tin.

Drawing Room Fruit Tarts with Crème Pâtissière

Use 1½ recipe of Pâté sucrée (page 41)

For crème pâtissière:

18 fl oz (500ml) full fat (whole) milk

2 vanilla pods, seeds removed and pods retained

6 free-range eggs, yolks only

4½ oz (120g) caster sugar

2oz (50g) plain flour

Toppings:

A selection of berries – blackberries, strawberries, raspberries

4 oz Apricot jam to glaze

You will need 12 small pastry tins with detachable bases.

Preheat the oven to 190C/350F/Gas 5.

Since the pastry will need to be baked blind, make parchment papers for 12 moulds. Grease the tins well.

Roll out your chilled pastry to 2-3 mm thickness. Line the cases with pastry, and cover with baking paper and beans.

Rest these in the fridge for 30 minutes to allow the pastry to firm up.

Bake them blind (*Line with baking parchment, and fill with baking beans*) for 15 minutes, remove from the oven. Paint each case with beaten egg, and return to bake for a further 8 minutes.

Leave to cool for 15 minutes, trim off the excess pastry, and lift out onto a cooling rack.

Next make the crème pâtissière:

Place the eggs, sugar, and flour in a large mixing bowl, and whisk until the colour alters and becomes a pale buttercup yellow.

Gradually add the warm milk and vanilla into the egg mixture, and stir well. Return the mixture to the pan.

Cook on a low heat until the mixture thickens, then pour into a clean bowl. Place a circle of greaseproof paper on the mixture. This will stop a skin from forming on the surface.

Once the crème is cold, spoon it into the pastry cases, and top with the fruit.

To give them a lustrous sheen, melt the apricot jam with 2 tbsp water, and paint over the tarts.

Leave to set.

Mrs Patmore's Yorkshire Curd Tarts

Remember Little Miss Muffett, eating her curds and whey? This recipe does exactly that, bringing a very old fashioned taste to the table. Mrs Patmore would have left the curds draining through muslin overnight, then set to making the tarts next morning.

Use 1 recipe of Pâté sucrée (page 41)

For the filling:

1.2 litres/2 pints full-fat (whole) milk

4 tbsp lemon juice

½ lemon, zest only

2½ oz (65 g) butter, softened

2½ oz (65 g) sugar

1 free-range egg, beaten

¼ tsp finely grated nutmeg

2 oz (50g) mixed dried fruit

Slowly warm the milk to a gentle simmer. Remove from the heat, and stir in your lemon juice. Leave to cool for an hour, and stir twice to help the curds to form.

Put the curds and whey into a sieve lined with muslin (cheesecloth), and drain the whey off into a jug overnight.

Roll out the pastry, mould to the tins, prick with a fork, and leave to chill in the fridge whilst you make the filling.

Cream the butter and sugar together until light, fluffy, and pale. Add the egg well. Mix in the curds, fruit, nutmeg, and lemon zest.

Fill the cases, and bake for 30-35 minutes or until the pastry is browned and the custard has set.

Allow to cool before taking out of the tin.

Downton's Finest Lemon Tarts

Use 1 recipe of Pâté sucrée_(page 41)

5 free-range eggs

4 fl oz (125ml) double cream (heavy whipping cream)

8 oz (225g) caster sugar

4 lemons, juice, and zest

Icing sugar, for dusting

8 loose-bottomed tart cases

Preheat the oven to 200C/400F/Gas 6.

Roll out the pastry, and line the tart tins.

Bake them blind ((*Line with baking parchment, and fill with baking beans*)) for 12-15 minutes, then remove the paper and beans. Trim away any excess pastry from the edges. Bake for a further 10 minutes until pale gold and completely dry.

Whisk together the eggs and sugar until light and fluffy. Mix in the lemons, and finally the cream. Using a jug, fill the cases, and return to the oven.

Bake for 18 minutes, or until the lemon filling is set.

Allow to cool for 30 minutes until taking out of the tin and dusting with icing sugar.

Yorkshire Apple Tart

1 recipe Pâté sucrée (page 41)

2 lb (900g) cooking apples, peeled and cored

6 oz (170g) sugar

Juice of half a lemon

1 tsp cinnamon

2 sweet apples, peeled, cored, and thinly sliced

Half a jar of apricot jam

Preheat the oven to 220C/425F/Gas Mark 7.

Roll out the pastry. Grease, flour, and line 8 tins with the pastry. Mould to shape, and prick with a fork. Set aside in the fridge whilst you prepare the apples.

Chop the cooking apples into small pieces. Add these with the sugar, and cook until mushy and all the juice has evaporated. Stir in the lemon juice and cinnamon.

Cut the sweet apples into quarters, leaving the skin on, but removing the core.

Slice the quarters very thinly.

Fill the cases with the apple purée, then arrange the apple slices prettily over the top. Since they will shrink, ensure they are well overlapped.

Bake for 18 minutes or until the apples and pastry look cooked.

Warm the apricot jam with 2 tbsp of water, sieve to clear of bits. Brush over the cooked tart as a glaze.

Leave for 30 mins. before removing from the tins.

MacClare Chocolate Tarts

1 mix Pâté sucrée (page 41)

14 oz (400g) plain chocolate, broken up

8 tbsp double cream (heavy whipping cream)

2 oz (60g) butter, cubed

2 tbsp caster sugar (optional)

Preheat the oven 190°C/380F/Gas 5

Roll the out the pastry, mould to the tins, prick the pastry, and chill for 30 mins

Bake the cases for 12 minutes until golden brown.

Melt the chocolate, butter, cream, and sugar together in a <u>bain marie</u>. Cook gently and thicken for 8 minutes.

Spoon the chocolate ganache into the cooked cases. Leave to chill and set.

Decorate with half a strawberry, and dust with icing sugar.

Dame Nellie Melba Custard Slice

1 recipe of puff pastry (page 43) or a pack of ready-made.

For the crème pâtissière

18 fl oz (500ml) milk

1 vanilla pod, split down the middle and seeds scraped out

3½ oz (100 ml) sugar

4 free-range eggs, yolks only

1½ oz (40g) corn flour (cornstarch)

1½ oz (40g) butter

For the icing

7oz (200g) icing sugar

5 tsp water

Preheat oven to 220C/425F/Gas Mark 7.

Grease two baking trays, and line with baking parchment

Roll out the pastry in two equal squares of 20 cm/8 ins

First make the custard:

Gently heat together the milk with the vanilla pod. Bring slowly to the boil.

In another large bowl, whisk the eggs, sugar, and corn flour.

Pour the warm, infused milk onto the egg mix. Stir well, and return to the heat.

Slowly bring it back to the boil, stirring continually. As it cooks, the custard will coat the back of the spoon.

As it boils, take it off the heat, and transfer to a clean bowl.

Cover with cling film, and leave to set in the fridge.

Place the pastry squares onto the sheets, and bake in a preheated oven until crisp and browned. This will take around 15 – 18 mins. Set them aside to cool.

When both pastry and custard are cooled, spread the custard over the pastry and add the top.

Flood with white icing, and return the cake to the fridge to set thoroughly.

Cut into 8 slices to serve.

Dough Buns

Jimmy's Finest Crumpets

12 fl oz (350 m) half fat (2%) milk, warmed but not boiling

1 lb (450 g) all flour

1/8 oz (5 g) dried yeast

2 tsp sugar

12 fl oz (350 ml) finger-warm water (tepid)

1 tsp Salt

1 tsp baking powder

Vegetable oil for cooking

Whisk together the flour, yeast, sugar, and milk, then add half the water. Mix until smooth, then gradually add the rest of the water until it is the consistency of thick cream.

Cover the bowl with a damp tea towel, and leave to rise for 2 hours until it is frothy.

Warm a frying pan, and coat thinly with a small amount of oil.

Using a small empty food can with both ends cut off to make a ring, put in in the pan, and pour the mixture in.

As the crumpet cooks, holes will appear on the surface. (If the mixture seeps outside of the ring, it is too thin, add more flour). This will take around 5 minutes.

Remove the ring, and flip to cook on the underside for two to three minutes.

Set on a cooling rack, and reheat under the grill or toaster when ready to serve with lashings of butter and some homemade jam.

Molesley's Toasted Tea Cakes

8 oz (225g) strong white bread flour

½ tsp salt

1 tsp fast action dried yeast

1 oz 15 g soft light brown sugar

¼ tsp freshly grated nutmeg

3 oz (75 g) mixed dried vine fruits (raisins, currants, sultanas)

2 oz (40 g) butter, melted

4 fl oz (120 ml) full fat (whole) milk, plus extra for brushing

Preheat oven to 200C/425F/Gas Mark 6

Soak the fruit in a cup of cold tea for 2 mins.

Mix together the flour yeast, sugar, and nutmeg in a large bowl.

In a saucepan, gently heat the milk and the butter, but do not allow it to boil.

Add it to the dry ingredients and the fruit, and then work until it makes a lovely smooth dough.

Turn out onto a floured surface, and knead for 5 minutes.

Divide into 8 balls of equal size and place on a lightly greased baking tray.

Cover with a tea towel, and leave in a warm place for around 45 minutes to rise to double the size.

Glaze the tops with milk

Place into a preheated oven, and bake for 15 minutes.

Remove, and cool on a rack

To serve, cut across horizontally, toast both halves, and flood with oozing melted butter.

Rosamund's Chelsea Buns

1 lb (500g) strong white flour, plus extra for dusting

1 tsp salt

1 x ¼ oz (7 g) sachet fact-action dried yeast

300 ml/10 fl oz (300 ml) milk

1½ oz (40 g) butter, softened at room temperature

1 free-range egg

Vegetable oil, for greasing

For the filling:

1 oz (25 g) unsalted butter, melted

3 oz (75 g) soft brown sugar

2 tsp ground cinnamon

5 oz (150 g) dried mixed fruit

For the glaze:

2 tbsp milk

2 tbsp caster sugar

To make the dough: add the yeast, flour, and salt together in a large bowl.

In a saucepan, warm the butter and milk gently, but do not boil.

Add together the milk mix and the dry ingredients, and combine together.

Turn out onto a lightly floured surface, and knead for around 5 minutes (adding more flour if necessary) until you have achieved a smooth dough.

Grease a bowl with vegetable oil, set the dough in, and cover with a tea towel.

Leave to rise in a warm place for around an hour or until it has doubled in size.

Lightly grease a baking tray.

Preheat oven to 190C/375F/Gas Mark 5.

Roll out the dough into a rectangle about ¾ inch thick.

Make the filling by melting the butter and adding the spices and fruit.

Smear all over the surface of the dough.

Tightly roll the dough and filling into a long sausage, like a Swiss roll.

Taking a sharp knife, cut the sausage into 10 slices.

Lay them onto the baking sheet, leaving space for them to rise between.

Cover with a tea towel, and leave to rise in a warm place for 20 minutes.

Cook in the preheated oven for 15 minutes.

Meanwhile, make your glaze by heating the milk and sugar to a boil, then simmering for 3 minutes.

Remove the Chelsea Buns from the oven, and paint with the glaze.

Place on cooling racks.

Serve at room temperature.

Rough cakes

Jos Tufton's Fat Rascals

Fat Rascals have been eaten in Yorkshire since the reign of Elizabeth I.

5½ oz (150 g) plain flour

5½ oz (150 g) self-rising flour

1 tsp baking powder

5½ oz (150 g) butter

5½ oz (150 g) mixed dried fruit

3½ oz (100 g) sugar

1 tsp cinnamon powder

½ tsp grated nutmeg

1 orange, zest only

1 lemon, zest only

1 free-range egg yolk

About 2 fl oz (50 ml) milk

For the glaze

1 free-range egg, yolk only

Pinch of salt

1 tbsp water

Flaked almonds and glacé cherries, to decorate

Preheat oven to 200C/400F/Gas Mark 6.

Lightly grease a baking tray.

Sift together the baking powder and flours, and rub together the butter and flour. Add in the sugar, fruit, zests, and spices. Little by little, add the milk to make a workable dough.

Divide into 12 small balls and flatten. Lay onto the baking sheet.

For the glaze, mix the salt water and butter together.

Sprinkle with cherries and almonds, and paint with the glaze

Bake for 15 -18 minutes or until browned and set.

These are served warm or cold and after with a big dollop of cream on the side.

Marigold's Rock Cakes

These Yorkshire favourites spread across Britain in the Second World War as they worked so well using rationing ingredients. These are sometimes also referred to as Drop Scones in other parts of the country.

8 oz (225 g) self-rising flour

1 tsp double action baking powder (US) or 1 tsp baking powder (UK)

4 oz (110 g) soft butter or margarine

2 oz (55 g) sugar

Pinch of mixed spice

4 0z (110 g) mixed dried fruit

2 oz (55 g) currants

1 medium egg

1 - 3 tbsp milk

Demerara sugar for sprinkling

Preheat the oven to 180C/350F/Gas Mark 4.

Lightly grease two baking trays, and line them with baking parchment.

Rub together the butter and flour until it resembles breadcrumbs.

Add in the sugar and fruit. Combine well.

Blend together with the beaten egg, and then drip the milk in little by little to make a damp mixture that will stick together.

Across the tray, drop 12 equal mounds, leaving space for them to spread.

Sprinkle over with Demerara to give a lovely dark crunch.

Bake in the preheated oven for 15 minutes.

Serve warm.

Charlie Grigg's Eccles Cakes

The Eccles cake actually comes from an hour's drive up the road from Yorkshire. Eccles, the town from which the cake is originated, is found in Lancashire. This rich, dark taste is one which one grows into, I think, a bit like coffee or whisky!

For the pastry:

1 recipe of puff pastry (page 43) or a packet of ready-made.

For the filling:

4 oz (120 g) currants

2 oz (60 g) butter

A few gratings of nutmeg

2 oz (60 g) soft dark brown sugar

1 egg white

Demerara sugar – for dusting

Preheat the oven 220C/425F/Gas Mark 7.

Roll out your puff pastry (page 43) to a rectangle of around 8 ins x 6 ins.

To make your filling, melt the butter, and throw in the sugar and spices. Leave boiling gently for one minute, then remove from the heat. You are looking for the currants to soften and the syrup to become infused with the spices.

Now roll out your pastry thinly, and cut out 12 x 10 cm/4ins circles with a cutter.

In the middle of each piece, place some filling.

Pinch up the edges of the pastry to seal the cake.

Turn over, and place the fastened side down on the baking tray.

Score three small cuts in the top of the pastry.

Paint with egg white, and sprinkle with sugar.

Bake your Eccles Cakes in the preheated oven for 15 minutes or until they are browned and risen.

Eat warm.

Ethel's Coconut Macaroons

2 large egg whites

¼ tsp cream of tartar

3½ oz (100 g) caster sugar

1 ½ oz (30 g) ground almonds

1 pinch of salt

1 teaspoon vanilla extract (or coconut essence if available)

9 oz (250 g) shredded coconut

Preheat the oven to 170°C/325°F/Gas Mark 3.

Grease and line a baking tray with baking parchment.

Whisk the egg whites to a very light froth. Add the cream of tartar. Mix in the sugar a teaspoon at a time. Now whisk the mixture until it makes very rigid peaks. If you have an electric whisk, this will save you the agony of cook's elbow!

Gently fold in the coconut, almonds, salt, and vanilla, taking care not to knock the air out of the meringue,

Drop 8 equal mounds onto the baking parchment, and bake for 20 mins until pale golden.

Carson's Sunday Afternoon Parkin

7 oz. (200g) butter, plus extra for greasing

1 large egg

4 tbsp milk

7 oz. (200 g) golden syrup (light Karo Syrup)

3 oz. (85 g) treacle (molasses)

3 oz. (85 g) light soft brown sugar

3½ oz. (100 g) medium oatmeal

9 oz. (250 g) self-rising flour

1 tbsp ground ginger

Preheat the oven to 160C/140C F/Gas Mark 3.

Grease and line a 9 in (22 cm) square tin, both base and inside.

Gently heat together the syrup, molasses/treacle, and sugar.

Mix together the ginger, flour, and oatmeal, then add them to the treacle mix.

Add in the milk, and then finally the egg.

Pour into your tin, and leave to bake for between 50-60 minutes. The top will be firm with a slight crunch. Use a skewer to check it is cooked right through.

When cooled turn out of the tin. Carefully wrap in foil to rest it for 3 or 4 days.

Try to resist the temptation to eat this too quickly as it gets stickier and more gorgeous the longer you leave it. (It will keep for 2 weeks in a tin).

Barrow's Lemon Bars

For the base:

6 oz (175 g) plain flour

2 oz (50 g) ground rice

3 oz (85 g) golden caster sugar

5 oz (140 g) cold butter, diced

1 tbsp milk

For the lemon topping:

Zest 3 lemons, plus 7 fl oz (200ml) lemon juice (about 4 lemons)

3 eggs

7 oz (200 g) caster sugar

1 oz (25 g) flour

Icing sugar, to dust

Preheat oven to 200C/425F/Gas Mark 6

Line 9 in (22cm) square tin base and insides.

Rub together the ground rice, flour, and butter, then add in the sugar.

Pour into your tin, and press down to make a solid base.

Bake for 15 minutes until a crust is formed.

Remove from the oven, and then turn down the temperature to 180C/350F/Gas Mark 4

Mix together the lemon and the eggs, and whisk together well.

Add in the sugar, and fold in the flour.

Pour the mixture over the base, and return to the oven.

Bake until the lemon is set, and leave to cool in the tin

Dust with icing sugar, and slice into 12.

His Lordship's Bram Brack

1 lb 5 oz (550 g) dried fruit - sultanas, currants, and raisins

4 oz (225 g) candied peel, chopped

8 oz (225 g) glace cherries (candied cherries), halved

10 fl oz (300 ml) cold, strong, black "Yorkshire" or other tea

150 g/5½ oz (150 g) butter, slightly softened

150 g/5½ oz (150 g) soft, dark brown sugar

3 large eggs

10 oz (225 g) all-purpose/plain flour

2 tsp baking powder

2 tbsp dark treacle/molasses

3 fl oz (100 ml) whisky

1 tsp freshly ground nutmeg

2 tsp lemon juice

4 oz (110 g) ground almonds

Preheat the oven to 170°C/325°F/Gas 3.

Grease and flour an 8 in (20 cm) round cake tin, base and insides.

Mix together the flour, baking powder, and spices.

In another bowl, cream together the butter and sugar. Add in the eggs, mixing together after each egg.

Mix in the flour, a third at a time, mixing well in between.

Drain the tea from the fruit. Add the fruit, treacle, lemon, nutmeg, whisky, and nuts to the mix.

Pour into the cake tin, and bake for 2½ hours or cooked till golden brown

Cool in the tin, then serve. Also keeps well in a cake tin.

Mr Bates' Treacle Tart

A teatime favourite to use up all of those crusts you have cut off.

1 recipe of Pâté Sucrée (page 41)

1 lb (450 g) golden syrup

3 oz (85 g) fresh breadcrumbs

A generous pinch ground ginger

1 lemon, zest, finely grated, and 2 tbsp of the juice

Preheat the oven to 190C/375F/Gas 5.

Grease a 9 in loose-bottomed tart tin.

Roll out your pastry, and line your tin

Line with baking parchment, and fill with baking beans. Bake it blind for 15 minutes.

Gently heat your golden syrup, add the ginger, and stir in your breadcrumbs.

Fill the pastry case, and return to the oven for 30 minutes.

Serve warm or cold.

Conclusion

I hope you have enjoyed your foray into the historical world of afternoon delicacies. I, as an English woman, would dearly love to see the tradition become popular again.

Perhaps in these days in which we are starting to become more aware of stress levels and haste through everyday life, the Afternoon Tea does, in fact, stand a chance.

How wonderful to think that perhaps, just even for one day a week, women may again be squirreled together around a pot of tea to share tales of their week and their dreams.

To my mind, that is the stuff where magic can begin; a delicious moment, a glimpse of real femininity as the root of a woman's power. What's more...all with a slice of cake!

That's it, then. I am going to leave you playing with ingredients in your head. As for me, I am off to the antique shop to invest in some silver sugar tongs and the very prettiest cake slice I can find.

And then....

Well, it's time for tea, of course!

Elizabeth Fellow

Definitions

Bain Marie – This is a two-tiered pot used for heating and melting ingredients over steam. It is possible to make an effective substitute by placing a bowl over a saucepan so the steam is locked inside and gently warms the contents of the bowl.

References and authorities:

http://imaginationlane.net/blog/historical-recipes-sandwiches-through-history/ - sandwiches

Disclaimer

Tea at Downton contains some traditional, some new, and some borrowed recipes which have been tried by myself. I have taken efforts to convey my recipe ideas correctly and to review each recipe carefully. Sometimes you may not get the desired results due to various factors such as quality of products, variations in ingredients, time taken in cooking and individual cooking ability.

Many of the recipes have been taken from historical books, and whilst I, as the author, was clearly not physically at an Edwardian Tea Party, these are traditional cakes and sandwiches which are true to the period.

The ideas published in **Tea at Downton** are purely based on individual opinion of Author. Please use them as a reference.

Lastly, **Tea at Downton** uses the names and references to the characters with thanks to ITV, but would like to stress is in no way affiliated to the programme or production team.

Check out other books
by Elizabeth Fellow!!!

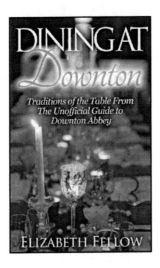

http://www.amazon.com/dp/B00Q79XRVC

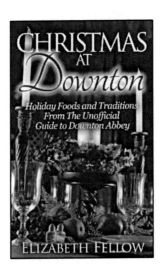

http://www.amazon.com/dp/B00P1RP9VM

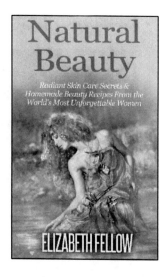

http://www.amazon.com/dp/B00KJKF8DU

http://www.amazon.com/dp/B00J914MMS

CPSIA information can be obtained at www.ICGtesting.com
Printed in the USA
LVOW06s1635221215

467520LV00021B/698/P